I0488184

SECRETS TO OVERCOME JOB DISSATISFACTION

MINDING *your own* G
BUSINESS!

SECRETS TO OVERCOME JOB DISSATISFACTION

Authors Choice Press
San Jose New York Lincoln Shanghai

Minding Your Own Business
Secrets to Overcome Job Dissatisfaction

Authors Choice Press
an imprint of iUniverse.com, Inc.

For information address:
iUniverse.com, Inc.
620 North 48th Street, Suite 201
Lincoln, NE 68504-3467
www.iuniverse.com

ISBN: 0-595-12967-6
Printed in the United States of America

TABLE OF CONTENTS

PREFACE

A friend received his notice of termination from his employer of the past ten years! He was stunned, shocked and hurt – *not happy!* His company had just experienced a merger and was downsizing and consolidating offices and management personnel. Still he was embarrassed and angry. "Why me?" he asked. I replied, "Why not you? Perhaps you have been given a gift; another chance to renew and begin something else! This is a new opportunity!" My advice, **don't ask "why?" Ask "why not!"**

It's a sad reality, but most people are *unhappy* in their work! My experience in career planning, education, sales and management have given me many counseling opportunities to share insights about *job satisfaction* with people who are in business for themselves, as well as with people who are working for someone else. My own life experience finding my niche in the work place has also taught me principles which can be employed to *achieve* job satisfaction. Many people, myself included, are victims of corporate downsizing, mergers, and a rapidly changing work ethic. That is what prompted me to write this book — a business person's self-help approach to therapy on-the-job. Understand that our relationships with other employees, management, and customers defines our business "family". These relationships must be based on *family values*, like *faith, trust, respect, honesty, and integrity.* **Only when we begin *employing* family values in the work place, can we begin *enjoying* our jobs and profiting from our work!**

Old business theories are obsolete. New business theory springs from emotion and spirituality! There is a rising discontent with the corporate system in America, especially its effect on ordinary employees. Dispirited by changing values, economics, and cultural customs, it's time to reclaim *your* entrepreneurial spirit to survive. *You* have an opportunity to be *your* own boss and love it! **Mind your own business!** Don't sell out to the agendas of other people, even when employed by them! *You* **are your own best customer and a part of all you earn is *yours* to keep!**

Pay yourself first! This book provides new perspectives for *you* and *your* business relationships. Enjoy higher dividends! "**Minding Your Own Business!**" is about overcoming job dissatisfaction and how to gain and maintain *your* own sense of value by employing and enjoying principles, practices, and concepts of integrity.

Don't blend in! This is about who you are and what you will become! It's telling you to be counted and to be accountable. It's telling you to be a participant and not remain invisible. It's challenging you to be extraordinary, accept leadership, and build your self-esteem.

Know that your perceptions and attitudes will determine your future! One of my favorite childhood stories is about two Goldfish Brothers who were members of the Carp Family, and lived in a pond in an enchanted woods. Reaching the ages when they must decide what to do with their futures, the Brothers Carp discussed with their parents whether to stay in the pond or venture further upstream to the larger lake that was just beyond the edge of the woods. One brother decided that he would stay in the pond he knew so well and grow up to be a big fish in a little pond. The other chose to leave the pond and venture into the lake beyond, where he could become a big fish in a bigger pond. Like the Goldfish Brothers, you too have life choices to make!

**"NO PERSON WHO IS ENTHUSIASTIC
ABOUT HIS WORK HAS ANYTHING
TO FEAR FROM LIFE."**
Samuel Goldwyn

PASSION

What's your Passion? How To Make It Happen!

A letter of recommendation was written for a gardener. The man wrote: "John Smith has an excellent knowledge for gardening. He knows how to cultivate the finest flowers and make a garden a thing of beauty." When the recipient read the letter, he concluded that this was the right man for the job! Then he noticed the three tragic words at the bottom of that page that ruined everything. "But he won't." While many people have all the qualifications to do a great job, they don't! **Quitters never win and winners never quit!** You can fulfill your passion. Do it! Passion compels us to act! Passion provides the motivation not only to do your job with excellence but really enjoy it! Hold yourself accountable; keep those high standards, goals and strategies your passion requires. There are two things to aim at in life: **"First to get what you want, and after that to enjoy it."** (Logan Persall Smith) Francois De La Rochefoucault commented that **"passion makes idiots of the cleverest men and makes the biggest idiots clever."** Passion is an attitude of the mind. Joseph Campbell describes passion as new action, aspiration, effort and vision. Choose to fulfill your passion! It's a sad reality, but **most people are unhappy in their work.** If they enjoyed it more they would be more successful at it. The secret is to figure out what you really enjoy doing. Ninety percent of what holds people back from achieving and realizing their passion is a personal ego issue. Think about it! Most of us want more challenge in our lives; more emotion; more passion! Don't surrender your passion, cultivate it! Patience, persistence, determination, and sacrifice are characteristics of passion. Make it happen!

**THERE IS A TENDENCY IN HUMAN
NATURE TO ULTIMATELY BECOME
PRECISELY LIKE THAT FOR
WHICH WE IMAGINE OR IMAGE
OURSELVES AS BEING.**

Fast food chicken King Colonel Sanders reportedly approached over one thousand restaurants before he finally succeeded in getting **one** restaurant to carry his chicken recipe on their menu. Thomas Edison tried more than ten thousand light bulbs before he invented **one** that worked! Abraham Lincoln over a period of twenty eight years, lost his job, failed in business and was defeated numerous times in his campaigns for public office before he was elected President of the United States. George Bernard Shaw wrote that **"when I was young I observed that nine out of ten things I did were failures, so I did ten times more work."** Jimmy Escalante, the mathematics teacher of East Los Angeles High School, helped his students pass the SAT tests with scores that startled educators. He simply kept telling his students, **"you can do it!".** Sir Winston Churchill encouraged a nation under siege during World War II to win the war with these words: **"never give up, never give up!"** All these men pursued their passion. Be exceptional, extraordinary, different and passionate! Film mogul Samuel Goldwyn once said, **"No person who is enthusiastic about his work has anything to fear from life."** Franklin Delano Roosevelt said, **"The only limit to our realization of tomorrow will be our doubt of today."**

**VISUALIZING A GOAL
IS LIKE WRITING OUT A
PROMISSORY NOTE
MADE OUT TO YOURSELF.**

PREPARATION

VISUALIZE: CONCEIVE IT, BELIEVE IT, ACHIEVE IT!

See yourself fulfilling your passions. Try preparing a poster size collage with pictures and words that are symbols of your passions. Frame your poster and display it where you will be subconsciously reminded of your goals on a daily, weekly and monthly basis. Say "YES" to your potential and write down your goals. Discuss "format" for a business plan with your colleagues or mentors. Experiment. Be sure to identify goals that are **S.M.A.R.T.** (Specific, Measurable, Achievable, Realistic and Tangible.) Develop a strategy of ways in which you intend to pursue these objectives. Make short-range and long-range plans. Review and revise your plans often. Did you know that there is a certain correlation between paper size used for outlining goals and their success in planning? Smallness keeps you confined. Use poster size paper to display your written or pictorial goals. Attend workshops that stimulate and excite you about making your personal business goals come alive. **Visualizing a goal is like writing out a promissory note made out to yourself.** Just as you write checks every day to pay for services rendered and merchandise purchased, write down your goals. **It's like writing yourself an installment check for your future!** The top 3% of achievers have written business plans. Dr. Norman Vincent Peal's book on "Positive Imaging" reminds us that whatever the human mind can conceive and believe, it has a good chance of achieving! Mental activity called "imaging" consists of vividly picturing in your conscious mind your desired goals or objectives. Hold that image until it sinks into your unconscious mind, there it releases great, untapped energies.

13

This practice works best when combined with the habit of **giving thanks for benefits before they are received.** "Visualization" is mental engineering. There is a deep tendency in human nature to **ultimately become precisely like that for which we imagine or image ourselves as being.** The metaphysician Neville once said, **"Acceptance of the end wills the means to that end."** Do not merely picture a hoped for goal, but instead visualize it with tremendous intensity. Hold the image of yourself succeeding, visualizing it so vividly that when the desired success comes it seems to be merely echoing a reality that has already existed in your mind. You are never defeated by anything until you accept the image of defeat. Great athletes use visualization. They often picture the technique that they see themselves winning an event in advance. The high jumper sees himself skimming over the bar. In the mind's eye of the athlete, he holds the mental picture of what he wants to happen in the next few seconds, before he makes his play. Intense concentration and focus of the mind helps us to achieve peak performances. The mental rehearsal of action puts the mind through a workout. Psychologists suggest that people can develop an "image bank" of various scenarios they can call on to help relax, to get motivated or to revisit their best moments to help build confidence. True passion is born of much self confidence and self esteem. Kramer's book, "How To Think and Grow Rich" suggests a system of six points:

1. Have a plan.
2. Write down your plan.
3. Know your plan.
4. Review your plan daily.
5. Be willing to make any sacrifice to achieve your plan.
6. Work on your plan.

14

Positive thinking or "possibility thinking", whatever you call it, is about practicing visualization and goal setting to achieve your passion.

POSITION YOUR DISPOSITION

The best defense is a good offense. A mysterious ancient Chinese warrior, philosopher Sun Tzu, compiled a book of military strategy over two thousand years ago entitled, "The Art of War". Sun Tzu believed that **"to overcome the enemy's armies without fighting was the best of skills."** The emotions of **fear, guilt, worry, anger,** and **stress** each present obstacles to achieving your dreams. Recognize and identify them as your enemies. Position yourself favorably toward them in order to confront and overcome them. You will accomplish this by being loyal to your ideals, standards, ethics and personal morals.

FACE YOUR FEARS. Fears are simply **F**alse **E**xpectations **A**lready **R**ealized. Fear causes panic. It paralyzes your will and your mind. Fear scares away money, people, and opportunities because fearful people are not creative, resourceful, or in command of their emotions. If people are afraid of you they won't talk frankly, and you won't know what is happening. It is easier to let things happen than to make them happen. Doing nothing rather than doing something is often the easiest path of least resistance and results in failure. Fight fear by identifying your greatest fears and confronting them. They are false expectations not true expectations. Replace those fears with positive expectations.

"WHEN A MAN BLAMES OTHERS
FOR HIS FAILURES, IT'S A GOOD
IDEA TO CREDIT OTHERS WITH
HIS SUCCESSES"

GIVE UP GUILT. "Guilt" is feeling bad about the past. Let bygones be bygones. "Guilt" is a useless emotion that creates negative stress. It lets you shift blame and allows you to abdicate control for improvement and change. Guilt is a penalty administered to make you feel bad. It is vengeful. Some familiar examples of guilt is the phrase that "you and your family deserve the best— implying that you should buy or face the consequences of letting the family down. Another favor- 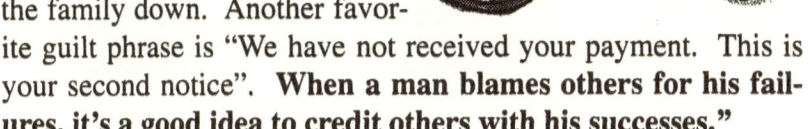 ite guilt phrase is "We have not received your payment. This is your second notice". **When a man blames others for his failures, it's a good idea to credit others with his successes."**

WIPE OUT WORRY. "Worry" is feeling bad about the future. Worries are fantasies about bad things the future may bring. If you are a worrier it only proves that you have an active imagination and exercise it regularly. Ninety percent of what we worry about never comes true and the few things that do come true cannot be prevented by worrying. Like a rocking chair, worry doesn't get you anywhere. Worry is a popular thing because for some it is a mark of caring, showing concern and being conscientious. Worry gives others an excuse for not taking constructive action. In the New Testament Jesus asks, **"Will all your worries add a single moment to your life?"** So why worry? Abraham Lincoln said,"The **best thing about the future is that it only comes one day at a time."** We need to take life one day at a time!

"THE BEST THING ABOUT THE FUTURE IS THAT IT ONLY COMES ONE DAY AT A TIME!"
Abraham Lincoln

ACT ON YOUR ANGER. Anger is drama. Anger can be a positive force to motivate change. Anger is both natural and inevitable. It can be channeled in healthy directions. Too often we use anger to blame the world and others for our not meeting our own expectations. Anger gets us off the hook! Raging anger is destructive when it translates into violent behavior. Listening to someone who is angry can diffuse the emotion or prevent it from escalating into violent behavior. Remember this powerful proverb, **"a quiet answer turneth away wrath."**

SAVE YOUR STRESS. Positive stress keeps you healthy, creative and active. Deadlines produce stress that help you get things accomplished. It can help keep you alert and enable you to perform your best. Most stress is learned behavior and can be *un*learned. However, stress has a negative result when your personal values take a back seat and relaxation, hobbies and diversions are sacrificed. Stress causes anxiety. Identify it and deal with it!

Your disposition is your best weapon to overcome "enemy" emotions without fighting. Work cooperatively, not competitively and pay attention to what's important. **Be hard on the issues and soft on people.** Accept the fact that emotions are normal and can be stimulating and productive agents of change in your development and achievements. However, if you allow enemy emotions to monopolize your life, the mind, body and soul will suffer.

19

**LEARNING MORE ABOUT
WHAT DOESN'T WORK, _STILL_
DOESN'T WORK!**

ATTITUDES OF THE HEART

The 1996 Summer Olympic game winners reaffirmed a common denominator among athletes that winners share in any professional field of endeavor. In addition to their natural skills of instinct and intuition, they practice discipline, set goals, have role models, and they are passionate. They share a positive attitude of the heart! **Always think about the possibility of winning, not the possibility of losing. Your passion makes your dreams possible! Learning more about what doesn't work, still doesn't work.** Nothing builds confidence and self esteem like the repetition of a superior performance. All good athletes know this. They learn from their successes! A golf pro chooses not to dwell on the unsuccessful shot. Babe Ruth is remembered for his home runs, not for his foul balls! Draw your strength and reassurance from your past accomplishments and successes. You have a positive past and a fantastic future. Be a winner not a whiner. The California lottery offers a dramatic example of possibility thinking by people who like playing against all odds. The odds for any one ticket will be nearly 223 million to 1. A person is twelve times more likely to be struck by lightning than to win the lottery and their chances of getting audited by the IRS are 1 in 6!

A father had two young sons. One was a total pessimist and the other, an eternal optimist. The father tried an unusual experiment to bring both boys into a more moderate attitude toward life. For his pessimistic son he provided a room on the top floor of his home that was flooded with sunshine from all directions. Inside were stacks of new toys that any boy would enjoy. Despite the happy environment his son began to complain that the room was too bright

**"EIGHTY PERCENT OF WINNING
IS SHOWING UP!"**
Woody Allen

and that he was growing tired of his toys. His other son, the optimist, had been given a room in the basement filled with nothing but horse manure and a large shovel. After several days in his new environment, he was overheard to say over and over, repeating enthusiastically, "with this much manure, there's got to be a pony in here somewhere!" Developing a positive attitude within yourself is all about growing up inside and balancing your mind and heart. John Milton wrote, **"The mind is its own place and it in itself, can make Heav'n of Hell, or Hell of Heav'n."** Attitude is a state of mind and your "mentality". **Before your future will change your attitude, your attitude will change your future!**

It is possible to shape your attitudes. You do this by being aware of a specific BIG PICTURE that includes an entire DNA of your future success. Follow the example of the Olympic athletes.

1. **SET GOALS.** Identify your goals. Be specific. Visualize them and write them down. Have a written plan. **Small commitments lead to large commitments.**

2. **SELECT ROLE MODELS.** Look around you and identify people who are successful, positive and focused. Study them. Be around them. Interact with them. Help them. Imitate them.

3. **PRACTICE DISCIPLINE.** Reebok sportswear company has a slogan they played over and over again on their infomercials during the Olympic telecast coverage. Their slogan was, **"Life is short. Play hard!"** In other words, get involved! Be counted! Woody Allen once said, **"Eighty percent of winning is showing up!"** Learn to be cooperative not just competitive. I would add, "Life is short. Play well!"

4. **SUPPORT OTHERS.** *"Do unto others as you would have them do unto you"*, is a timeless proverb of encouragement. This Golden Rule leads to gold! Practice the principle of "karma", the notion of cause and effect. "Karma" means being aware that your choices and actions in the present will boomerang to you in the future. You cannot afford pessimism and negativity because it is life threatening!

5. **BE CONFIDENT.** Eliminate "wimp" words such as "try" and "can't" because they will defeat your ambition and resolve.

PRACTICE

DEVELOP YOUR MENTAL MUSCLES

Ants are strong and they are wise! In every country in the world, the ant is proverbial for "industrious". They store and collect their food for future use. There is abundant evidence of their social and military organization. In fact they take and train their slaves. Ants have elaborately constructed nests and in some cases practice a sort of agriculture. Like the story of the ant, develop activities and exercises that will empower and stimulate your intuition. Improve your communication skills, enrich your self esteem and increase your self awareness to enable you to adopt an attitude that will encourage productive growth and stimulate your mind. I call these "power tasks" that give you a mental workout.

1. Read
2. Take mental breaks
3. Focus on fitness and nutrition
4. Take cultural adventures
5. Write down your problems
6. Control your workplace environment

Know that every thought you have also stimulates a psychosomatic, spiritual, emotional and intellectual change and reaction in your body! Everything begins with a thought. What you focus on will expand. "Endorphins" are chemical substances released in our blood streams that may have a physiological or physical effect. For example, most athletes have experienced a "runners high", thought to be caused by the release of "endorphins".

READ, READ, READ the RIGHT STUFF and the right way! Television has given us an alternative to reading and we have become lazy. Educate yourself so you can educate others about yourself, your services and your job. Our favorite bonus product that we can offer ourselves is information. Don't be dull; read newspapers, magazines, books and even movie subtitles! Explore the Internet and be inquisitive!

TAKE MENTAL BREAKS by engaging in activities that involve the non-rational part of your mind, such as a creative pursuit like painting, gardening, physical exercise, or meditation. Practice meditation as a form of mental relaxation. Detach yourself. Spend a few minutes each day focused on deep breathing exercises and quiet moments that can help you enter a state of relaxed alertness.

FOCUS ON FITNESS by exercising vigorously and often. Under movement can lead to physical disorders such as heart disease, hypertension, over weight, depression, apathy, and lethargy. Pay attention to diet. Some foods act directly on the brain. For example, caffeine and refined sugar. Each person reacts differently to different foods, but be informed that **"each food has its poison, so balance your poisons."** Experiment with foods that offer you the best nutrition.

TAKE CULTURAL ADVENTURES by traveling and experiencing different climates, people and customs. Go to the theater, concerts, museums, parks and stimulate your senses and mind.

WRITE DOWN YOUR PROBLEMS and this simple act will solve many of your problems because it will distract you from worrying about them.

CONTROL YOUR ENVIRONMENT and create a mental gymnasium at your workplace. By making your office a climate where everyone can improve their "mental muscles" it becomes a place that is also inviting to you. You will appreciate that it offers opportunities to pick up and develop new skills and knowledge and provide a place for you to practice those skills. Each day you will have grown in some way. Over time, if you use the workplace to your fullest advantage, you become a high achiever. It will also demonstrate to you that you are not really working for the boss, but rather working for yourself!

"GOD HAS WISELY GIVEN US TWO EARS AND A MOUTH SO WE MAY HEAR TWICE AS MUCH AS WE SPEAK."

Epictetus

LISTEN-UP

Three old timers living in a retirement community were seated on a park bench. One of them said to the other, "It sure is windy today." "No", said the other, "It's Thursday." "I am too!", said the third man, "Let's go get a 7-Up!" Not everyone absorbs input at the same rate, or retains it. Most of our learning occurs through our five senses of sight, touch, smell, taste and hearing. Listening involves mastering verbal and non-verbal communication. We remember 80% of what we do. We remember only 50% of what we see. And we only remember 10% of what we hear! My father has a favorite saying that **"it is sometimes better to remain silent and be thought a fool than to speak up and remove all doubt!"** The Greek philosopher Epictetus put it in a different way by saying, **"God has wisely given us two ears and a mouth so we may hear twice as much as we speak."** Miscommunication is the root of most misunderstanding. Hearing a "no" is as important as hearing a "yes". In order to take the next relevant steps in making progress in our communication with another person we must qualify the relationship we have with the other person. If we hear a "no" then we must pause and handle the resistance.

"Objections" are windows of opportunity to ask more questions. And, the person who asks the questions controls the communication. Objections are merely concerns that haven't yet been resolved and are therefore opportunities to render service and offer remedies. An objection is not equal to a rejection. It is only a request for more information! In order to overcome objections and

SAYING NOTHING IS OFTEN BETTER THAN SAYING JUST ANYTHING.

continue a dialogue, a good listener will probe the unconscious and ask, "what it is that I need to know that will help me that you haven't already told me?" Active listening is facilitated by forming a relationship between the person doing the talking (the teacher) and the person listening (the learner). Enhance your sense of control and competence by *listening* to the useful information and *ignoring* the rest. The talker (teacher) must be encouraged to express feelings, criticisms and ideas , and the listener (learner) must be able to give attention and practice retention of what is being said. The listener (learner) must also be able to accept criticism in order to overcome resistance. The most important thing you can do to *win* is to let the other person (the teacher) present their entire argument *without* any *interruptions.* This will suggest that you *want to listen* and will calm the complainer. Active listening must invite action, probe and encourage new information by answering a question. Motivate by offering acknowledgment and praise. Make the other person be honest and feel accountable for their words. Have you stopped listening?Do you speak for others often **before** you find out what they really want? The listening device most unused is "silence". **Saying nothing is often better than saying just anything.** A simple pause can motivate the talker to volunteer valuable information. "Mirroring" is imitating the speech patterns, tonality, pace and intensity of the speaker.(teacher) By mirroring another's response, it can also be an effective device in winning the confidence, trust , acceptance and attention from the person (teacher) to whom you are listening. **Six ways to listen better include:**
1. Focus on the speaker's eyes and mouth.
2. Visualize the speaker's words.
3. Take some notes.
4. Ask questions and don't interrupt.
5. Eliminate distractions.
6. Listen with your whole body; sit up straight, nod, and maintain eye contact.

"COMMON SENSE IS NOT SO COMMON."
Voltaire

GENES AND GENIUS: PLAY YOUR HUNCHES

Attitude not **aptitude** will determine your future! Some very smart people do some dumb things. Many people with only average IQ's run their lives quite successfully. **Instinct** and **intuition** are our natural skills. We each possess them, although we are not equally in tune with our inner feelings. This phenomenon is called our "gut feeling" or "common sense". Voltaire remarked that **"common sense is not so common".** Common sense is what is often obvious and a simple solution. Louise L. Hay calls that *place* of intuition the "voice within". It's the "ding" that sounds off in your head which for some inexplicable reason we know to follow. This occurs because your thoughts shape your future. You possess a God-like ability to know the difference between what is right and what is wrong. Your inspiration is the result of an awakening of a spiritual, intuitive knowing because of your connection with a higher mind. Dr. Deepak Chopra describes this "knowing" as a "kernel of being that doesn't change—a spark of divinity — where infinite potential resides." Joseph Campbell describes this phenomena as following one's bliss. It is nothing more or less than taking a risk. As you accumulate life's lessons and experiences you develop your awareness of this inner spiritual center and deep within you it speaks more clearly and louder as a mechanism for self expression. Some call it "ESP", our extra sensory perceptions and powers. You are born with this gift. Unless you learn to be a risk taker, you cannot learn to use this skill. **Play your hunches!** Self-trust plays an important part and underscores your ability to meet with change. Develop your *practical* intelligence to reason and logically solve problems as well as your *intuitive* intelligence to understand and respond to events. Learn to recognize what your *initiative* intelligence is telling you and to use your rational mind to evaluate the message so that it can help your intuitive mind work more efficiently. When there is no objective evidence for your beliefs, it can interfere with sensible thinking *unless* you can accept that you learn from your imagination as well as from actual experiences. Intuitive thinking can often provide solutions to problems too complex to analyze rationally. When logic fails you, then you must find your own way to explore *other* means. Believing in something for which there is no objective evidence is also called "esoteric thinking" or "practical" intelligence. Play your hunches! Don't be afraid of losing or failing. Face the risk and possibility of failure. Be prepared to accept the consequences! Your life won't last forever, but at least it will be a life you canl be proud of!

PERFORMANCE

AVOIDING MENTAL BANKRUPTCY & BUSINESS BURNOUT

Simplify your life! Streamline your schedule by making life easier. Achieve accomplishment without exhaustion. In California, everyone who owns and drives an automobile, which is practically everyone, is concerned with keeping clean driving records in order to keep their driver's license and also more importantly, to keep their insurance rates lower. Traffic schools have flourished in the state because people eagerly enroll in order to avoid being penalized with a poor driving record. A driver is allowed to attend traffic school once a year to keep a moving violation from being reported on their driver's record. The traffic school phenomena in California is also noteworthy because these schools seek to entertain as well as to instruct, making an otherwise boring experience fun and bearable. The traffic school business is highly competitive and to attract customers they have adopted names like "Express-Way Comedy School", "Improv Comedy Traffic School", "The Entertainment Traffic School" and the "Less Stress Traffic School:". Some traffic schools feature magicians, films, videos, live entertainers and comedians to entertain their customers. This marketing approach is certainly a creative approach to overcome a boring but necessary task. It is also an example of how we can reinvent our jobs to make them more stimulating and rewarding!

Accept accountability. Many of us have become "cry-babies" and are playing the "blame game" - blaming unfulfilled achievement on the *other* guy or the system. It is the age of the all purpose victim. We are all victims of past economic abuse. We have over extended our credit and leveraged away our profits. An individual, or a group's plight, condition, or monetary setback is excused and defended on the basis that we as individual's have lost control. Personal accountability means that problems can be solved by an individual effort and initiative. The problem is that a person and society at-large cannot operate if everyone has rights and no one has responsibilities. We live and work in a pluralistic society. Different groups, companies and individuals have different family and cultural values and traditions. Today an attitude of New Age arrogance promotes the belief that "you can have it all!" There is a balance!

Today, people are filled with a sense and expectation of entitlement or the "I Deserve It" syndrome. What this is really saying is that you deserve "better". You deserve "honesty" in business and "value" in your life.

There are many examples of abuse of our delicate and fragile society which cut across economic and ethnic boundaries. Leona Helmsley, Keating , O.J. Simpson, and Milken are examples of newsmakers who would compromise and betray the rules and morality to serve selfish gain. Our courts and system of justice have been abused by a corps of legal bureaucrats, lawyers, and politicians who don't practice justice, but do contribute to the chaos and confusion of our law and the administration of this justice. We each share the burden and opportunity to participate in our national and personal wellness. If you don't agree with your office and company's values — then help to change them.

Your ideals, values and standards must be expressed, respected and appreciated- and not merely tolerated. It is important to develop a family culture, and acceptable way of doing things. This will define the behavior and character that is acceptable.

Develop a professional family team. Team management, team sales, partnership and group leadership all increase productivity one and a half times! Teams must share common goals. Team players must learn not to compete with their partners. And the "team" approach will also **prevent "burnout"** by making life easier and improving distribution of tasks. Some ways to develop a winning team include:

1. Learn how to help others become successful.
2. Play to win.
3. Do the right thing!
4. Take risks.
5. Care about other team members.

OVERCOMING DYSFUNCTIONAL OFFICE
FAMILY DIVERSIONS

Two young women who had formed a highly successful sales team asked their manager to discuss and mediate the break-up of their partnership. This meeting proved highly successful. Each woman continues to be a valued participant in that office. They have remained friends and each are now enjoying a successful business pursuing separate new directions. Another office crisis involved a successful salesman who had decided he could no longer work in the office unless another agent was fired, whom he felt to be dishonest and unethical. This salesman had taken it upon himself to circulate a petition to terminate the other agent. When confronted by his manager for his actions, he gave an ultimatum that either the other agent would have to go or he would leave the office. The manager gave this matter considerable thought and attention. The agent was invited to work through the process and attempt to diffuse his anger and hostility. Given the choice of either staying and finding a solution, or leaving if his demands were not accommodated, he left. While the office manager respected his right to disagree, he did not agree that the end result the salesperson desired justified his means to achieve that result. It proved to be an important test of the manager's leadership. As a result of his decision, the manager received the approval and support of the other office family members.

ANTICIPATE CONFLICT AND CONTROL IT WHERE YOU WORK. This is the key to overcoming dysfunctional behavior within your professional family. We are developing extended

**"IT MARKS A BIG STEP IN YOUR
DEVELOPMENT WHEN YOU
REALIZE THAT OTHER PEOPLE CAN
HELP YOU DO A BETTER JOB
THAN YOU COULD DO ALONE!"**
Andrew Carnegie

families through teamwork to realize our common and individual goals and objectives. Support groups, networking groups, task forces, and management by committee are important examples of this. **Professional family conflict and disputes are normal, unavoidable, and important** because they are necessary **catalysts for individual growth** of the family members. Family members learn to define identities and boundaries where the "me" ends and the "we" begins. But family disputes can be unhealthy when they are not managed well, and they infect or transfer anger and hostility towards the other members of the professional family. Develop a process where "family members" can communicate openly. **Care about the success of every other member.** Andrew Carnegie once said, **"It marks a big step in your development when you realize that other people can help you do a better job than you could do alone."**

Things you can do to encourage open communication:

1. Encourage **intimacy** because it will invite trust, empathy, and caring. Intimacy is bonding, and does not cause a loss of privacy and freedom.
2. Negotiate disagreements.
3. Learn and listen; tolerate and talk about needs and feelings.
4. Take time to talk and listen to another point-of-view and do not expect to resolve everything at once or forever. This is realistic and healthy.
5. Solve easy issues first!
6. Demonstrate equity and fairness.
7. Strive to make commitments and goals for the family that are constructive, obtainable and realistic in order to reinforce competence of the individuals.

8. Avoid commitments and goals that are idealistic and which only reinforce an individual's weaknesses.
9. Recognize that "trust" and "integrity" are the key elements to a healthy family atmosphere.
10. Be forgiving.

These practices will encourage solidarity within the family. A conflict free professional family is not possible, because familiar issues tend to recur in every person's life regardless of gender and age. A signal is that we hear a "cry for help" or an **"S.O.S."** These "Signals **Of** Struggle" that trigger conflicts are:

1. Power and control. Who gets to decide?
2. Competition. Who gets privacy, privilege, attention, acknowledgment and praise?
3. Autonomy. Who will give up some independence?
4. Threat of loss. Who will react to the separation and loss of someone who is leaving or threatening to leave the office family?
5. Betrayal. Who will feel betrayed by broken promises and concessions not kept?
6. Unrealistic expectations. Who expects too much and expects perfection in an imperfect world?

New divisions in our society make it necessary for us to reinvent and re-emphasize **family terms** like **"tender, caring, patience, nurturing, support, belonging, loving, trust, integrity, and forgiveness."** Our society is no longer a "melting pot" but rather we are becoming smaller, polarized groups with fewer things in common. For example, in the office place we have smokers versus non-smokers; men versus women; corporate managerial types versus entrepreneurial types; blue collar versus white collar.

While we must allow for diversity and individuality, we must also identify values that create a common bond. The fact is that **what we do have in common are much more important than our differences.** We have common needs to be loved, appreciated, recognized, praised, and counted on. We share a need to be included, missed, the need for friendship and the need to belong. We share a need for a job, a home and for someone to care about us. We share a need to be a part of a family and the need to make a difference! Praise, acknowledgment and encouragement are key ways to finding a successful outcome. **Remember to celebrate effort, regardless of outcome!**

**YOUR CUSTOMERS DON'T CARE
HOW MUCH YOU KNOW UNTIL THEY
KNOW HOW MUCH YOU CARE!**

PROMOTION

PERSONAL MARKETING:
THE ART OF SELF PROMOTION

The most important — and least well-executed element of being successful is personal marketing. You must sell yourself by **putting others first!** In order to sell yourself effectively, you must determine what it is about yourself that makes you a valuable ally and will endear you to others! **Your customers don't care how much you know until they know how much you care!** Customers today want special attention. If they perceive that they are special to you, they will return to you again and again to get that special attention. They will even pay a higher price for it! Your customers need to feel that having **you** will enhance the quality of their life. Customers buy products and services that benefit their appearance and the way they feel about themselves. Most people want to associate with other people who look good, feel good, have style, dignity, and good reputations. The worst mistake to make in marketing yourself is to ignore or argue with your customer. The idea that the "customer is always right", the "customer is King", and "put the customer **first**", are American business values based on the concept that your customer wants you to **make them feel important**, and that you care about their comfort and well being. In Europe, service is always "correct" but not always friendly and caring. Americans, on the other hand, have high and often exaggerated expectations of service.

45

BEFORE SOMEONE WILL BUY *FROM* YOU, THEY WILL HAVE TO BUY *INTO* YOU!

Success in today's work place depends on initiative and action, not reaction. The "hard sell" approach has lost its grip. The successful people today are the ones who use the kinder, gentler type of approach. A new business person has emerged because the customer has changed. People today are more savvy, less gullible and not so easily convinced. Intimidation is a method of the past. "Probing", a planned process of questioning and active listening, is the key to successful personal promotion because you can learn what your customers want from you. Personal virtues such as honesty and integrity are the best PR marketing tools in today's information age because **people want to know more that you care about them than what you know!** Selling yourself today requires a soft sell. Ask for business and ask permission before you act!

Be they colleagues, associates, employees or the public, once you have identified who your customers are and their needs, then you can begin to promote yourself by offering them benefits. People will tell you their needs in descending order from the most important to the least important, if you ask them.

The **benefits** that are **most important** to people are:

1. Making money
2. Saving money
3. Saving time
4. Avoiding conflict
5. Personal comfort
6. Being popular
7. Receiving praise and recognition

8. Having fun
9. Being in style
10. Avoiding criticism.
11. Avoiding trouble
12. Independence; expressing individuality
13. Good reputation
14. Gaining control over their lives
15. Personal safety and security.

Above all else, you need to understand and appreciate that **you are in the marketing business.** The basis of all great marketing is built on the unselfish desire to "do good" for your customer. It's impossible to provide too much service. **Before someone will buy from you, they will have to buy into you!** This decade is being called the "needy nineties" because people need to feel special and unique. They need assurances that you have compassion, tolerance, ethics and integrity. You need to create an active partnership with your customers by identifying their unfulfilled needs and meeting them. We are now in a new decade of social conscience. Ethics, passion, service, compassion, integrity and basic honesty are "hot"! Glitz, hype, moral bankruptcy are "not"!

It's a time of making sacrifices for the future, prompted by our desire to survive. **Truth in advertising** and **total disclosure,** about ingredients in food products and drugs, toxic and hazardous substances in products, environmental hazards such as asbestos, gasses, waste and disclosure of potential problems from cars to contracts and houses are all manifestations of this new social awakening. Be able to state the **benefits** that you can offer others. It will give you a compelling advantage!

PEOPLE PERSUASION:
ACT AND DRESS TO IMPRESS

Modern plastic surgery procedures such as breast implants, nose reconstruction, tummy tucks, hair plugs, hair extensions, and liposuction are all done on perfectly healthy bodies to signal a better message to others! Cosmetic surgery makes us look younger for longer because **we need to stay competitive in the work force longer.** Economics require us to work harder and longer. **Most of us can't afford to feel or look our age! We must improve our appearance to stay competitive in the job market.** You need to impress others that you are fit for the future in order to extend your earning power. Be concerned about your appearance, your diet and the food you eat, as well as your exercise to build strength and stamina. This is not just for the sake of vanity, it is for survival! Few of us can expect to depend on social security or pension funds for our golden years! Making judgments about people based on external signs is common to most societies and cultures, ancient and modern. Your outward badges can determine your place in the social hierarchy. In this country, **55% of what we believe about another person is based on our observation and interpretation of nonverbal signals.** Many people are looking for reasons to eliminate you from competing before you have a chance to impress them with your usefulness. This includes all the peripheral elements of appearance, accessories, hair care, skin care, make-up, grooming, positioning and posture. Together these "badges" project an image of credibility, stability and power as well as individual style.

55% OF WHAT WE BELIEVE ABOUT ANOTHER PERSON IS BASED ON NONVERBAL SIGNALS.

A generation of Baby Boomers (ages 32-50) who once exclaimed, "Don't trust anyone over 30" now want to change the business attitude about the implications of aging. The Boomers are those 76 million Americans born in the years from 1946, when births exploded above the 3 million level for the first time through 1964 – the last year before births showed a decline. Boomers have *saved* at only a third the rate they will need to maintain their current lifestyle in retirement. Therefore, *they must stay in the work force longer.* Dr. Robert Arnot, a physician and TV commentator, authored a book "Guide To Turning Back the Clock" that proposes a combination of diet and exercises to restore aging bodies to the state they were in during their 20's. Plenty of Boomers subscribe to the myth of eternal youth.

**PEOPLE RESPOND EMOTIONALLY
BEFORE THEY RESPOND
INTELLECTUALLY.**

BODYTALK: SHOW YOUR TRUE COLORS

My five year old niece can talk up a storm when at home with her family, but she becomes absolutely silent when approached by a stranger. In these situations, she talks with her eyes, with a nod or her head, or a beautiful smile. **Body language** is the very **first** language we use in the beginning years of our lives. Then, we gradually add speech. So, it makes perfect sense that our communication now embraces a combination of verbal and non-verbal behavior. **We are actually held more accountable for our word than our body language, yet the irony is that when one contradicts the other, we tend to believe the body language!** Two aspects of the body language that are of special interest are "territory" and "positioning". Greater importance is being placed on personal contact with our associates and our customers. We like to meet each other, hear each other's voices, have eye contact, shake hands, and see each other's movements. To gain "involvement" and not intrude is the objective of a handshake or the reason for passing an item onto another person. A confident manner and movement is a trustworthy protective device. Nervous gestures are ways of reducing tension and calming ourselves, but they are often detected and perceived as showing weakness. The power of visual expression means that your total appearance says more about you than the verbal message you deliver. People judge books by their covers. Likewise people are often judged by their appearances, actions, conduct, and reputations. Accept it! This is because **people respond emotionally before they respond intellectually.** Use clothing, appearance and props as tools to create the response you want. It is by your actions, and not your words that you establish morale and integrity. You cannot say one thing and do another!

Whether or not you consider yourself a salesperson, the first thing that ever gets sold is you! Product and company affiliation are secondary. The good news is that looking professional and looking good is a skill that can be learned by anyone who wants to learn it. Marketing yourself visually is a skill that can be learned! Nowhere is fashion, grooming and appearance more decisive as a tactic than in a courtroom where a defendant can use clothes, props and appearance to sway a jury. Psychologists at Jury Behavior Research, Inc., in Los Angeles, conduct witness workshops and charge lawyers and their clients by the hour for advice about everything from dress, to body language, to speech patterns. While image experts and attorneys agree that ultimately, evidence matters more than what the defendant wears, "little" things do effect the jury enough so that lawyers have learned to employ subtle tactic to manipulate perceptions of the jury. In the celebrated O.J. Simpson case a slight of the hand with a glove prompted the Defendant's attorney Johnny Cochran to exclaim, "If the glove doesn't fit then you must acquit!" Those jurors admit they were influenced by the use of this prop. In business, many people dress above their position, trying to create the impression that they are destined for better things. They usually *are* if they have the ability to back up their look. Body presentation skills are among the most important skills to be learned in non-verbal communication.

It is a fact: body language is important when communicating with others. But as clearly as our bodies may be speaking to others, it may be saying something to you! If you are feeling off balance, then perhaps your body is sending the message that *change* is necessary. Feeling lost or confused? This message may be telling you to seek *spiritual* nourishment that only prayer or meditation can satisfy.

POWER

POWER PARANOIA: DON'T BE INTIMIDATED!

Henry Ford once said that **"if you believe you have the power, then you have it. If you don't think you do, then you don't."** The contemporary American style of power is to pretend that you have none. Most people do not like to admit that they want power and **that** is exactly why they never get it! The instinct for power is basic to men and women, but it is usually thought of as one of mankind's less attractive characteristics, along with aggression and violence. **Power** gives us the opportunity and the stability to act or produce an effect and make a difference! It provides us with a vehicle by which we can persuade others and administer authority and control over others. Understanding "power" is important **because power undermines every purpose and principle for our working.** "Power" by definition, implies moral vigor, physical might and authority. Leaders and power brokers must be capable of emotion and behave well. We must learn to administer power to be our servant and not our master. We must take our jobs seriously, but not take ourselves too seriously. Ernest Hemingway called it **"grace under fire"** and John F. Kennedy once called living with power as living with **"grace under pressure."** Living with power is not an easy task. Absolute extreme power almost always absolutely corrupts. Leading people without making them subservient should be our goal in establishing powerful relationships and it is our key to empowering ourselves. Michael Korda, author of the book, "Power: How To Get It, How To Use It" offers the definition

"IF YOU BELIEVE YOU HAVE THE POWER,
THEN YOU HAVE IT.

IF YOU DON'T THINK YOU DO,
THEN YOU DON'T."
Henry Ford

of "power" I like most. He defines power as **"the ability to bring about our desires."** **Working for power is one of the principle reasons for our working.** The other reasons for working include: **working for habit, pleasure, money** and **meaning.** In business, working for power provides us with influence. Working for habit gives us self-discipline, order and meaning, and it provides us with an inner sense of control and confidence. Working for pleasure keeps us busy and gives us a sense of worth, belonging and value. Working for money justifies our reasons for exacting a "tribute" of a monetary wage from others. Money is our reward and sometimes the reason we work because of the purchasing power it provides. **Power, habit, pleasure** and **money** are all **motivations** for our working. The **rituals** of power techniques employed by the powerful are usually performed in the public view. They are almost always territorial. Few power players are at ease in other people's offices and tend to like meeting on their own turf or on a neutral ground. Power is implemented by **techniques** like the practices I have described in this book. And power is displayed by **symbols.** Symbols of power include colors, clothes, cars, office, location of desk, car phones, body language, positioning, posture, physical appearance and attitude. Power symbols are often cultural and will vary accordingly.

You can apply some of the characteristics of powerful people to acquire and use your powers. I have used the acronym **"HOPEFUL"** to describe 7 of the most important characteristics of powerful people.

"THERE ARE NO HOPELESS SITUATIONS; THERE ARE ONLY MEN AND WOMEN WHO HAVE GROWN HOPELESS ABOUT THEM."
Field Marshall Fosh

Hope is a power that energizes us with life, excitement and anticipation as we look to the future. You can live 40 days without food; 4 days without water; 4 minutes without air; but only 4 seconds without hope! Hope transforms obstacles into possibilities. Napoleon once said, **"A leader is a dealer in hope."** Field Marshall Fosh, hero of Verdun in WWII said, **"There are no hopeless situations; there are only men and women who have grown hopeless about them."** Powerful people are hopeful! **"Where there is no hope in the future, there is no power in the present."** (Dr. John Maxwell)

Organized. Powerful people organize their resources. They map out a strategy that will lead them towards their objectives.

Passionate. Powerful people are passionate. They discover a reason, a consuming, energizing almost obsessive purpose that drives them. They do not take the adversities of life and accept them as limitations. They have strong beliefs about what they want to accomplish and why.

Energetic. Powerful people have vibrancy, charisma and vitality.

Fundamental judgments. Powerful people have a clarity of their values about what is important and what really matters to them! They have made fundamental ethical, moral and practical judgments about what they want and they have decided that they are willing to pay the price!

Understanding. Powerful people have in common an extraordinary ability to bond with others and to develop rapport with people. They have an ability to communicate and connect. They have developed a mastery of verbal and non-verbal communication.

Learned. Powerful people are prepared with the facts and have accumulated information, knowledge and experience to use as *their* resources.

DON'T GET ATTACHED TO THE OUTCOME!

WOMEN AND POWER

The 1993 United Nations Human Development study of women's worldwide status in the workplace reported that the number of women in the work force has soared to 42% in industrial countries and 34% worldwide. However, the jobs they hold are generally lower status and lower paid. "No country treats its women as well as it treats its men." Women fight stereotypes!
This report states that "women are the world's largest excluded group. Even though women make up half the adult population, women make up just over 10% of the world's parliamentary representatives and consistently less than 4% of Cabinet ministers or other positions of executive authority." In fact, only 15% of women executives report having had a female mentor or role model. "Sexism" has been a difficult obstacle to overcome. However, the influence of women in the nineties also differs from earlier decades. The reasons for the rise in female power and influence is connected with the public's dissatisfaction with the way things are. Women are seen as *different*, and therefore good. Women are often perceived to be more honest and caring than men. And because of these reasons, women approach their power differently than men. A brief examination of this important difference will help you to understand and not underestimate this dynamic. Women have advantages! Men seldom are inclined to see women as rivals. Most men tend to underrate women. For example, most men tend to talk too much and naturally confide in women. Intelligent women can exploit this habit. It is also a fact that men will do almost anything to avoid a face-to-face confrontation with a woman. Therefore a woman is well advised to insist on a face-to-face encounter with a

man rather than doing business by fax or memorandum. Another advantage is that a woman can usually sit anywhere she pleases and position herself in a power position at almost any meeting! Women tend to fight harder. Women make concessions that men do not make. For example, a woman often postpones having children for her career.

Do not confuse "power" with "control". You can over exercise your control of people and situations. Stop helping so much unless asked. Don't "micro-manage". *Let* other people make mistakes and experience hard knocks. This will help them to become functional, strong, and more flexible. Empower others! The object of power is to avoid opposition and not to provoke it. People who know how to use power start by making sure all obstacles are cleared from their path. Give the other person some control. Don't waste energy seeking to contol or change other people. Give up the need to convince and control others. People want to come to their own conclusions and they want to be the first to think of a solution. Make it happen by giving power as well as exerting power. In this way you put our focus on the *process* and not the *outcome.* To acquire power you must relinquish your attachment to it. When you spread responsibility you also spread risk. When you share credit you receive parise and credit. **Don't get attached to the outcome.** Practice "acceptance" by letting other people be who *they* are!

AVOID EXPLOITATION WITH NEGOTIATION

In the ancient days, there was a certain beggar who had begged rice and moved to a position outside the city gates to cook his meal. While making his fire, he heard an advancing caravan. He quickly moved toward the city gates. "Alms, Alms, " he cried, and more loudly when he saw a Prince approaching. The Prince stopped at the gate beside the beggar and said, "What have you to give me for the alms I might give you?"
The beggar clutched his 25-30 grains of rice in his fist and offered only 3 grains to the Prince. The Prince took the 3 grains of rice and held them for a moment. He then took the Beggar's hand and carefully laid the 3 grains of rice in the moist palm of the Beggar's hand and folded his fingers over them. Leaving the Beggar, he then moved onward to enter the city gate. As the Beggar walked back to his fire, he opened his hand. To his amazement, there lay 3 brilliant gems alongside the 3 grains of rice. The Beggar gasped and then wept, "If only I had given him all!" **"If you give a little, you will get a little in return."** (The Bible, Corinthians, Chapter 9 verse 6). **"Even God doesn't give with both hands!"** Each action has a cost in exchange for a reward.
Negotiations trade favors. A good relationship is both equitable and profitable. Profit results if the rewards or benefits are greater than the cost. An inequitable relationship is when one person profits and the other side incurs a loss or gives something away with no measurable reward. Successful negotiation involves changing behavior and not people. Self interest will determine a person's behavior and the outcome of their negotiation. Negotiation must reward people and make the reward tangible, immediate and specific.

**"IF YOU GIVE A LITTLE, YOU WILL
GET A LITTLE IN RETURN"**
<u>The Bible</u>, Corinthians, Chapter 9, verse 6)

Philosophic promises of future benefits do not offer tangible rewards – and will depreciate quickly. People will only change their behavior if they understand the consequences of changing their behavior. The *reward* is exchanging behavior or attitude for a reward or benefit. Aesop's fable of the stick and the carrot still applies. The way to change attitude and conduct is by using reward "carrots" to quickly reinforce success. Jerry Jellison, author of the book, "Changing the Leopard's Spots" suggests that we trade one favor at a time. He calls this a "specific reward system." Timing is an important consideration to be given before you negotiate. The best time to ask for a favor is when other people need something from you and you can offer an exchange. The worst time to make a request is when you need a favor but have nothing to offer in return.

Negotiation means solving differences and overcoming objections. Negotiation requires working *cooperatively*, not *competitively*. The common objective of negotiation is to bridge differences and balance various competing issues in order to arrive at a common understanding. **Be soft on people and hard on the issues.** Generalize rather than personalize your argument, using situations, numbers, theories, principles and data to support and explain your reasons. There are two primary styles of negotiation. They are:

1. The Competitive Approach
2. The Cooperative Approach

The **competitive** style is the hard sell, inflexible approach. It places

**BE *SOFT* ON PEOPLE
AND <u>HARD</u> ON THE ISSUES.**

people on opposite sides of the issues. It creates a hostile and threatening climate. People tend to speak in terms of *absolutes* and are inflexible. Deals are lost over small points and ego "personal issues".

The **cooperative** style is compassionate and sensitive. It is characterized by good listeners who pay attention to what's important to the other person. "He who speaks first loses" is not always true! The advantage of speaking first is that you can accept and shape the expectations of the other side. Decide which side is "selling" and which side is "buying". A seller's expectation is the "sticker price" that tells the "buyer" they won't be asked to pay *more* than the sticker price. Artful negotiations determine the settlement. A buyer's "offer" only tells the seller that the "buyer" will not pay *less* than their opening offer. **All business today focuses on benefits!** We are constantly selling, trading and exchanging benefits. The underlying motivation for negotiation is determined by the "cost" versus the "reward" of negotiation and compromise. Some of the most persuasive reasons to negotiate are the **benefits** listed below:

To make money	To save time
To avoid conflict	To gain comfort
To be recognized	To conserve possessions
To increse enjoyment	To enhance individuality
To emulate others	To avoid criticism
To avoid trouble	To exploit opportunities
To protect our reputation	To gain control of our lives
To feel safe and secure	To increase enjoyment
To gain praise	To be popular
To be in style	

GENERALIZE RATHER THAN
PERSONALIZE YOUR ARGUMENT

As a successful negotiator you must recognize how to avoid being exploited! Here are some rules to follow:

1. Never open your negotiations with something you cannot afford to lose.

2. Recognize when you are negotiating in a competitive environment.

3. Be forgiving. Be *soft* on people and *hard* on issues.

4. Be clear about your willingness to cooperate.

5. Never make an offer, which if accepted, you don't want!

6. Do not negotiate purely from your reliance on intuition and instinct. Train, practice, discipline, rehearse, listen, and follow the example of others. Ask for support and give support in return!

Negotiation is a *process* and It can be *learned*!

"FAITH IS THE SUBSTANCE OF THINGS HOPED FOR, THE EVIDENCE OF THINGS NOT SEEN."
The Bible, Hebrews, Chapter 11, Verse 1)

SPIRITUAL SOLUTIONS FOR
BUSINESS SITUATIONS

A pig and a hen walked side by side down a country road while engaged in a philosophical conversation. The hen said, "Why don't we treat our good neighbors to a free breakfast? I'll provide the eggs and you provide the bacon." Replied the pig, "Wait a minute! To do that would only require of you a contribution, but from me it requires a total commitment." Total commitment requires faith. **"Faith is the substance of things hoped for, the evidence of things not seen."** (The Bible, Hebrews, Chapter 11, verse 1) *Faith* is **giving thanks in advance for the right outcome!**

Faith is based on trust in yourself and belief in others. It is easier to have faith in others when you first have faith in yourself. Faith is demonstrated by your actions. It is by your actions, not just your word, that you establish credibility, morale, integrity, and a sense of values. You cannot say one thing and do another! Applying spiritual orientations brings an attitude of harmony to all that the day brings. Our mind can be filled with right solutions, which increase our awareness of God and His blessings because we become co-creators with God. We should believe that we have "unlimited" power to effect positive changes in our lives – and that infinite abundance is already ours by right. Jesus said, "Anything is possible if you have faith." The Bible, Mark, Chapter 9, verse 23. "Trickle-down economics", as described by our modern day politicians, is based on a theory of scarcity – that resources are finite and our wants and needs are infinite. On a personal level, the belief in scarcity fosters feelings of insecurity and encourages greed. Overcoming spiritual insensitivity and mediocrity is your greatest personal challenge! Thinking spiritually will help you to transcend the profit motive by giving reassurance that in addition to profit, there is a mental and spiritual enrichment motive for working. We should reach into our inner well of spirituality and discover our "humanhood", recognizing our common human frailties and imperfections. Then, we can reorganize our priorities and recognize that we are all "family". Actions of "love" and "caring" should be recognized as motivators in the work place. Put "people business" first and replace rigid, hierarchical structures with more flexible networks. Empower people to make decisions on their own, spur creativity at all levels and promote company wide and office ownership of results. You approach finding a spiritual solution in the workplace by taking quiet moments for contemplation. Prayer and meditation is a silent affirmation of divine guidance and peace. "Peace" is the ability to stay calm in spite of the panic of unpleasant or chaotic, stressful circumstances. The reward of meditation is finding a deeper knowing, an inspired vision or intuitive revelation. We cannot deny that our business goals are also rooted in spiritual overtones. We build family businesses, build monuments, write books, produce films, create art, establish trust foundations and contribute to philanthropic, charitable organizations, in our attempts to insure and preserve our memories. We are fascinated and obsessed with how we can achieve for ourselves a measure of immortality. A measure of immortality is our effect and contribution to the lives we touch in our daily pursuit of our dreams and passions knowing that we can make a difference!

Knowing *the meaning of life* improves the quality of our life. It extends our survival as well as motivates us to claim our futures!

Reorganizing the spiritual aspect of our lives helps us to fully appreciate our humanhood. We come to the conclusion that we are human beings *first*, with a greater potential for living life to its fullest.

There is a breed of eagle which every seven years goes through a ritual that is contrary to the rules of survival in the wild. The eagle flies to a high, desolate place on the side of the mountain and there begins to pull out the strong wing feathers which are the very source of its flying and its means of finding food for survival. When the wing feathers are pulled out, the eagle begins a still stranger procedure. It breaks off the talons that have served it to grasp food, or to hold it secure on some high lofty perch. Bedraggled and defenseless, the eagle is a mockery of its once proud self; but it is not through yet! The beak is next to go! On a jagged rock, the eagle grinds its great beak until only a nub is left. After a few weeks, a strange transformation begins to take place. New and stronger wing feathers grow and new claws now replace the split and broken old talons. A sharp new beak has formed to replace the chipped and nicked old beak. The eagle has been renewed and regenerated! With greater strength the eagle now leaps from the mountain to soar again, up,up in the sky and goes higher than ever before! It is possible that even the proud creation, man, must sometimes become helpless in order to be renewed and to climb higher than ever before!

A salesperson approached his manager with a request. Having successfully negotiated a $3 million plus sales transaction for a celebrity client, there was yet one important contingency required for the sale to close successfully. The salesperson visited the manager

EVERY POSITIVE THOUGHT
IS A PRAYER!

in his office to ask him to pray for his client so that his work would be rewarded. The manager prayed. A day later, he heard that the client was having a new problem with an important deal point. He prayed harder. Two days later, he called the agent to inquire how things were and the agent excitedly told him that a phone call had just come that morning with news that his clients had removed their final contingency. The agent thanked his manager for his prayers! It was especially meaningful to his manager that the agent had enough faith in his spirituality and example to invite him to use prayer as a sales tool! Prayer is a powerful force! **Every positive thought is a prayer!** A power passage from the New Testament Book of James encourages us **"to pray for each other so that you may be healed. The earnest prayer of a righteous man has great power and wonderful results."**

The essence of Christian spirituality and in fact the fundamental meaning of most of the world's religions is the principle of unconditional love. Love comes from God by God's grace and is bestowed, not earned. Our ability to love our neighbor as we love ourselves must begin with coming to terms with our own reality, fallibility and humanhood, as well as our spirituality and immortality. Here are some spiritual suggestions to follow:

1. **Pray**, meditate, think of reasons before you act. Experience *yourself.* Spend some private time considering your actions and motives. Think of the alternatives that may result. New Agers call this "treatment" the act of making positive "affirmations."

2. **Stop playing God.** You cannot do everything! Get yourself a confidant or support group. Practice teamwork, tolerance and forgiveness. Forgiveness can heal and revitalize emotions. Recognize the need for giving and receiving forgiveness!

**"... CHRIST IN YOUR HEARTS
IS YOUR ONLY HOPE
OF GLORY."**
The Bible, Colossians, Chapter 1, Verse 27

3. **Live in the moment.** Derive pleasure from the present. Be free to enjoy the company of a loved one, a star filled sky, a poem, a flower, or a terrific meal. Approach life with a childlike sense of wonder and awe. Have a vision for the future! Empowering yourself with a sense of spiritual sincerity will provide you with an emotional stability and enable you to distinguish between short-sightedness versus long term business decisions. Balancing your spiritual nature will provide you with another important business barometer in achieving your vision.

We are created by God to express spiritual attributes. Within each of us is the Christ spirit that fills us with the drive and encouragement needed to reach our goals. Anything is possible with the spirit of Christ, if we believe. The Apostle Paul writes in The Bible, **"God has kept this secret for centuries and generations past...".** And the secret is simply this: **"...that Christ in your hearts is your only hope of glory."** (The Bible, Colossians, Chapter 1, verse 27) **God's mighty energy is at work *within* you!**

You will discover that acting skillfully on your higher values brings no penalties! To the contrary, it will enrich you to feel more fulfilled knowing that your actions are dedicated to a higher purpose.

**"LOVE THY NEIGHBOR AS THYSELF,
BUT CHOOSE YOUR NEIGHBORHOOD."**
Louise Beal

PROSPERITY

ACHIEVE YOUR DREAMS WITH SELF ESTEEM

Elephant trainers shackle young elephants with heavy chains attached to deeply embedded stakes. A young elephant learns to stay in place. Older elephants never try to leave, even though they may easily have the strength to pull the stakes and move beyond. People are like these elephants. We can learn through conditioning. We are prodigies of our cultural climate and we are shaped by our business environments. A healthy work place and work ethic is the key to our ability to achieve our dreams and strengthen our self esteem. **You are who you work with!** Louise Beal once said, **Love thy neighbor as thyself, but choose your neighborhood."** A veteran of Southern California real estate, I have learned that one of the most important factors that contributes to property value is "location". There is a saying that property value in Southern California is determined by "location, location, location!" Your professional destiny is also shaped by your "location" and affiliation with the right organization and people. The office or company "culture" is a set of values and ways of behaving that are common in a community and tend to perpetuate themselves. These values become our behavior norm. **Values that emphasize the importance of people are values that create a process for change.** Take culture into your own hands. Tradition is not enough! Question everything! Writer George Orwell believed that an individual's rights and feelings would always rise above any theory, plan or procedure. He wrote of the decency of the common man trying to do the right thing! Make up your own mind as to what is right or wrong and stand by it. Any culture that has no room for differences will only be a repressive culture and unhealthy environment. A culturally healthy person is a wealthy person. The wealth may not be in the bank, but **you** can bank on your potential because you will be empowered by your vision and confidence to produce accomplishments.

Every group that works together develops a culture. "Culture" is not a string of pearls, but it is the sum total of all the ways people agree to act to achieve a common objectives and a system of values they can follow.

To illustrate how some specific cultural values differ in the workplace, consider some contrasting examples how Asians, Hispanics and Anglos traditionally perceive the following:

self sacrifice - to be expected (Asian)
    perceived as good (Latin)
    considered to be unhealthy; unnecessary (Anglo)

authority -   to be obeyed (Asian)
    to be respected (Latin)
    to be questioned (Anglo)

time -   not specific (Asian)
    vague; relative (Latin)
    precise; "time is money" (Anglo)

family -   family more important than individual (Asian)
    family most important (Latin)
    individual more important (Angelo)

80

achievement - achieve for honor (Asian)
relationship oriented (Latin)
achieves for emotional or material reward (Anglo)

emotion - downplayed (Asian)
important to express (Latin)
downplayed (Anglo)

You must embrace change in order for your office culture to change. Change is a *destination* and not a single happening or *event*. Change involves developing new business strategies, plans and vision as well as the recruitment of new talent and the retention and training of experienced personnel. Change is a process that never ends. Office, companies, organizations and individuals begin to deteriorate when they cannot integrate change into their cultures. Past success can tie us to the past and cause us to become too conservative to change or be experimental. This leads to poor results. Our individual and collective success will suffer an identity crisis if we fail to recognize and embrace new business theory. Some practical tips on how to implement change and invigorate your customers and colleagues include:

1. Sell new ideas .

2. Adopt a culture of teamwork using task forces, committees, focus groups and symposiums at your office to encourage sharing ideas and responsibilities.

3. Strive for excellence and leadership by becoming more efficient and more powerful.

**SPEND MORE TIME LOOKING
OUT FOR PEOPLE THAN CARING
ABOUT HOW YOU LOOK TO THEM.**

4. Strive for diversity and balance. My staff personnel don't look alike, think alike, or have the same personalities, but all of them share the same objectives and goals. Allow for diversity, individuality and creative expression. Don't be a clone and avoid cloning others. Be tolerant of different styles and differences of opinions.

5. Put people first! Be a people person. We are all in the relationship business. We need to be "people friendly". We need to structure relationships that will produce results for us by networking with peers and subordinates. The *people networks* that we create will be of critical help whenever we go through a period of crisis. **Spend more time looking out for people than caring about how you look to them.** Talk about your concerns with the people you learn to trust . Use them as a sounding board. Find and use mentors. Don't become isolated! Control your office climate. Contribute to creating a climate of positive high energy, cooperation and concern for the other person. Instill commitment by rewarding competence and maintaining consistency.

**"A PART OF ALL YOU EARN IS
YOURS TO KEEP"**
From the book, "The Richest Man In Babylon"

PROSPERITY

EARN BONUSES WITH PERSONAL BUDGETING

A book, "The Richest Man In Babylon" tells the story of a certain man who was famous for his great wealth and generosity. Even though he was very generous to others, each year his own wealth increased faster than he could spend it. One day some close friends came and asked him to share his secret so they too could accumulate great wealth. They made a bargain. The richest man in Babylon agreed *to tell the secret of his success* if they kept their bargain. The secret he shared was *this*: **"A part of all you earn is yours to keep."** You accomplish this by **taking care of yourself and being accountable.**

Pay yourself. *This is the secret.* Be good to yourself and move away from negative people whose attitudes will tear you down! Practice the principle of "exclusion" or getting rid of negative people and negative thoughts around you. Negative people and thoughts are expensive and costly baggage. Emotionally, we are attached to *attitudes* more strongly than we are to material *things* and *possessions.* Our habits shape our attitudes about ourselves, other people, and our relationships with parents, children, co-workers, careers, marriages, and our jobs. Negative thoughts have the neurological ability to attract to them similar negative thoughts.

Budget your time! You've heard the saying, **"Time is money"**, and so it is! Budgeting your time can be accomplished by implementing a system of prioritizing productive time versus non-productive time. Rather than looking at the bottom line, the dollars

**MOST PEOPLE FAIL IN LIFE BECAUSE
THEY MAJOR IN MINORS!**

and cents, consider instead focusing on "time" as an alternative precious resource that you can manage. People and personal relationships are your resources for advancement, increased sales, and your key to independence. Identify your customers by putting people first! **Who you know, and who knows you** is your ticket to success in the nineties! This is the information age and information is cheap as well as available at every Fax or personal computer terminal. So instead, **focus on people** and how you can spend *more* time with them! There are 3 classifications for budgeting your "time".

1. **Productive Time** is *actual time spent* in face-to-fact contact with another person who is your customer. This "customer" may be your boss, your staff, or another associate.

2. **Indirectly Productive Time** is the time you spend making a direct *effort* to arrange a face-to-face contact with your customer.

3. **Non-Productive Time** is *everything* else. "Non-Productive" time is not *un*important *time*, because it includes your errands, phone calls, preparation time and learning situations.

Create a "list" of things to do. In your daily planner, label or rank your activities and tasks accordingly. Daily and weekly planners include daily goals for which we must allow time.
Only 18% of people working are spending more than 20% of their time productively. Your objective should be to spend 1/3 of your time equally divided between *productive time, indirectly productive time*, and *non-productive time*. Prioritizing your activities and tasks is a simple formula that will enable you to better analyze

and review your schedule. *Budget* your most valuable resource - *your time*!

Investing in yourself includes allowing yourself to play, have fun and rest. Even sleeping can be a form of investment if done for the sake of *future* activity. Leisure activities or play can involve a genuine investment of the self.

Prioritize! Most people fail in life because they major in minors. Time management also involves organization and being able to distinguish between important material versus junk material. Don't be a collector, saving everything that comes across your desk.

Keep your old contacts! You can budget your time by keeping your existing customers and business associates. It costs you many times more (estimated between to one hundred times) to develop *new* customers, friends and associates than to maintain and nurture existing ones.

AFTERWORD

**"YOU WILL KNOW THE TRUTH AND
THE TRUTH WILL SET YOU FREE."**
Jesus Christ

AFTERWORD

"Minding Your Own Business!" is about standing up for yourself with dignity, self-respect and being comfortable with your life's work. It is a business person's approach to therapy on-the-job. Not all of us want to own a business. Not all of us have the talent, opportunity, financial resources, ability, or the inclination to own a business. But you can take responsibility for yourself and enjoy the benefits of determining your own destiny. These concepts are revolutionary for your future! You must know that you are free to be yourself! The truth is that **your chief want in life is somebody who will make you do what you can!** Mankind has a savior complex. We look for someone to give us the *secret* to the meaning of life. Our heroes are men and women who have achieved entrepreneurial celebrity. The real truth is *that* somebody is yourself! Jesus said, **You will know the truth and the truth will set you free!"** You have all the resources within to heal and change anything.

In an ancient time, when God was creating mankind in God's own image and likeness, God called a meeting of His heavenly company. All the top Angeles and Archangels were invited to attend because God wanted their opinion on a very important and urgent matter. God was considering giving his creation, Mankind, a very special gift, *"the secret of life"*. But God wanted to know where He should hide this precious treasure so that only the most deserving and earnest of men would be able to find it. One Angel thought it should be sunk in the depths of the sea. Another thought - God should bury the *"secret of life"* deep in the earth. Yet a third Angel thought this secret should be hidden near the sky, high on a mountain top in a desolate region of the earth. But a fourth Angel had a different opinion. "Mankind will be a tricky breed," said the Angel. "Someone will swim to the depths of the sea. Another will dig deep into the earth. Somebody will surely climb the highest mountain. Therefore God should place the *"secret of life"* someplace where Mankind would *never* dream of looking for it - right *inside* of man himself!" God nodded in approval at the wisdom of this Angel. And so it was done! You possess this most precious gift right inside of yourself - your *spirit*, your *attitude*! You have all the resources within and without to heal and change anything. Don't fight it- use it! The importance of a non-resistant attitude to overcome anything that appears to be threatening was emphasized and demonstrated by great men throughout history. Jesus Christ, Ghandi, Martin Luther King and Caesar Chavez all knew that the way to of overcome adversity is by standing firm! By standing firm in the midst of trouble and confusion you can reaffirm and exercise your unlimited spiritual capacities of peace, strength, and self-assurance.

ACKNOWLEDGMENT

I wish to acknowledge a number of special people who have contributed their time and talent to this writing project. They include the people with whom I've worked and shared professional bonds, both past and present, and for whom I care. They are my inspiration for this material. They are my teachers, and I have chosen to be their messenger.

I thank James Hancock for his encouragement and belief in my abilities to undertake this ambitious task. I thank my parents for their support and enthusiasm. I thank my brother Rick Mathis and friend Boots Clements for their skillful editorial guidance; Wendy Callister for her valuable help and endless hours at the word processor. I also acknowledge Jeff Vernon (graphic artist), Ted Jewell (caricaturist), and David Massoud (printer). I thank my friend Richard Christian for his encouragement to self-publish. Most especially, I thank God for an eventful life that has taught me important lessons I can share with others. Finally, I thank the readers who buy this book and use these ideas and principles to enjoy a better life!